"I may be lame in my hip but I am not lame in my brain"

Faith and Accountability brought me to Victory

George Valentine Peterson
10/23/2014

George Valentine Peterson

Dedication

To my dedicated wife Irene Peterson, thank you for inspiring me to share my life's Journey.

Foreword

To all individuals who are experiencing a handicap, this book was written with you on my mind and in my heart. I believe and I am a witness that you can succeed and overcome obstacles if you are determined not to allow them to become the controller of your inward person. To my family, friends, former co-workers and all individuals: it is my sincere hope that my story will inspire, motivate, enlighten and empower every creed and color to do something worth your years of living, and deserving of aging with grace and dignity.

Acknowledgements

I would like to express my gratitude to Teresa Johnson, Jerome & Courtney Lawrence (Pastor and wife) also Sharon Lawrence, Maxine Hunt, Paulena Gresham, Monica Williams, children, grandchildren, family, church family and friends. Special thanks to my friends Mr. Rodion Eglevsky, Gene Eglevsky and my nephew Ernest Anderson and family. First contribution to my book given by Rodie, thank you.

TABLE OF CONTENTS

Chapter One - The Apple of my eye

Chapter Two - Childhood lessons

Chapter Three- School Time

Chapter Four - Electronics, TV's and radios

Chapter Five - Learning from the best

Chapter Six - God is always with me

Chapter Seven - NASA

Chapter Eight- Giving back

CHAPTER ONE

The Apple of My Eye

As was told by my father, it was snowing on February 14, 1926 when my mother Ann Scott of Redbank, New Jersey, gave birth to twins; my sister and me. My mother had not been very well during her pregnancy with us. She became even more ill during her labor. Because of the long struggle with life and death from our birth, she finally answered our gracious Lord's beckoning call, and crossed the endless journey of life to enter into His paradise. I never got the opportunity to meet my mother. She made a great sacrifice, and endured physical ailments that finally ended after my sister and I were released from her life's span. Later on in life as we grew older, my father told my sister and me that our mother gave him blessings and best wishes for himself and to raise their twin babies.

My father was David Isaiah Peterson. He was born and raised in Saxon Woods, New York. I was told by my father that after my mother's death, he was very heartbroken and sad.

My father experienced sadness over the loss of his wife and mother of his now twin children. It was somewhat difficult to truly be happy to raise two children without their mother.

My grandmother realized that my father had to find a home for us and a half-brother named Bobby. So my father decided that his best option was to place us with his parents; Eugene and Julia to raise us on their small six acre farm.

My aunt Beulah, of Scarsdale, New York lived with us too. Living with my grandparents on the farm was more enjoyable with aunt Beulah there. Aunt Beulah was deformed from birth by being slightly hunch back. She was single and didn't mind helping my father to care for us. She accepted us twins with a true mother's love. I still remember the children's Lord's Prayer that she taught us.

My grandmother Julia of Richmond, Virginia was a Christian and loving grandmother. She strongly believed in not sparing the rod and spoiling the child. This is an attribute which I think is needed today. When we needed discipline, we got it. It gave us something to think about before we got into mischief again.

In my opinion, she was a great grandmother and a true disciplinarian. She disciplined us with love and always hoped we would learn our lesson from whatever mistake we made. I truly missed her during my young adult life.

My grandfather, Eugene Peterson was a hardworking man. He strove to provide for us all. Even though he worked long hours and sometimes on weekends, he always seemed to make some time for my sister and me. As a young man my grandfather moved to Scarsdale, New York, with his new bride Julia to work a farm that he purchased. He made a living building twenty-six miles of bridle paths for John D. Rockefeller. My grandfather cleaned most of the farmland in the area with saw axes, a brush cutter, and a team of horses.

I can still remember during the time of the depression around the year of 1931, my grandfather sharpening his tools. He was a firm believer that it was not a sharp tool that injured an individual but a dull tool. This was why one of the things he really made sure of was that all of his tools were sharp. Even today I follow this example.

I remember him smoking a pipe. Later in my life, I started the same bad habit. I became a pipe smoker myself and smoked for forty years. I believe that seeing my grandfather doing it and it seemed enjoyable to him was the reason I began to smoke a pipe. I know for sure that influence is a powerful force whether it is good or bad; and people have a choice in the matter. My grandfather was certainly a role model to me. There were times when he would have "spirit time". During this period, he would go over to the wall or into the woods and make little bows and arrows for my sister and me to play with.

He enjoyed being alone at times building and making things. I recall one time my uncle Alford had bought a 1931/32 Ford, and he was outside polishing it. I went outside with a hammer in my hand and I guess I was just being an active little boy and started hitting on the fender of his automobile with the hammer.

I am sure I was not thinking about any damage that it could cause. Well, he caught me hitting his new Ford. Uncle Alford wanted to really give me a good spanking on my rear.

I remember my grandfather stopped him and said to him, "how that boy handles that hammer he's going to be an engineer or somebody great someday."

My uncle certainly didn't see this nor was he thinking about me being an engineer either. I didn't get the spanking that I probably should have. I was told to put the hammer up and to not ever hit my uncle's automobile or I would be in big trouble. I didn't want to get in trouble. I don't recall ever doing that again.

I can still remember the beautiful fruit trees blooming in the spring down at 299 Saxon Wood Road where my grandparents lived and farmed. It was one of those sights that was very hard to forget; seeing cherry trees, plum trees, and other fruits blossoming. My grandfather had a beautiful grape harvest too. At times during the fall of the year when he was in the mood, he would make wine from the grapes of his land. Some of their old friends would come over and sip wine with them. My grandfather had barrels of wine in his basement and he would extract it from the barrels. I gathered that this was something that most all of the old farmers around there did. They sampled each other's wine. I remember my grandparents would tell me not to go up and pick apples in the apple trees and, as with all children, it went in one ear and out the other ear. One day while outside playing, my sister and I decided to climb an apple tree that was behind the house.

As I reached an apple, my foot slipped and I fell. My right foot got caught in a "v" shape around a tree limb. I was hanging upside down, crying and scared. I was really afraid; first because my leg was hurting really bad and second because I knew I was in big trouble. My sister ran and got my grandfather. He had been working in the barn. He and my grandmother came running to help me out of the tree. I was told that I had been hanging there for about five to ten minutes. Afterward, my grandparents took me in the house and they noticed that my leg was swollen and bruised. I was really hurting. From that day on, my leg would always bother me to the extent that I started limping on it quite a bit. This was during the early summer, and everyday it was getting more difficult for me to walk correctly.

I remember my grandfather had a little brook that ran through his farm. He said he would block it up and make it like a little swimming pool for my sister and I to play in. One day while we were playing, I got into the cold water. It was a very hot day and my sister and I were playing in the water. We had fun too, but my leg began to hurt really bad again. I believe that getting into the pool was certainly the prelude for contracting polio in my right leg. After my right leg kept swelling my grandparents knew that something was seriously wrong. I had started limping more and more.

My grandmother tried old-fashioned remedies like rubbing liniments and other stuff on my leg but my leg did not get better. Consequently, I started dragging my right leg more and more. Finally, they decided that they needed to call my dad and tell him about my injury. They told him that I had climbed the apple tree and while I was falling, my leg got hung around a limb, and that they thought I needed to go to a doctor soon because the remedies they had tried weren't helping and they didn't like the way I was walking.

My father came down to see me. He examined my leg and he agreed with my grandparents that it would be wise for them to contact a doctor to see what the actual problem was.

When my father came for this trip he brought a distinguished lady with him whom I learned later would become my stepmother. Her name was Viola Winslow. She was a widow. Viola was very tall and big bosomed, with straight long red hair and a most pleasant smile. Her skin was white. From what I learned of her background, her parents were from Halifax, Nova Scotia. They were of Gay-Head Indian, French, and Negro ancestry. It seems like the genes had turned towards the white side of this three-way relationship which made it somewhat complex because she always had to let who ever she contacted know who she was and what she stood for. I will assure you that anyone she met would know that she was probably one of the blackest white women they ever knew.

Today I think of many of the things she taught me, and how she stood beside me as a young boy in the hospital. I remember going through many operations on my leg where they did bone transfer to my hip. One time I remember I lost all feeling in my right leg and they stuck needles in it to see if I felt anything. My right leg was not growing like my left leg. They strapped me to an operating table and put my right leg into something that looked like a halter – something like you would put on a horse. It had a special device attached with which they attempted to stretch my leg. **This was probably one of the reasons why I limp much more than I should today because the leg finally grew even after it was stretched.**

My father worked every day. He was burning garbage at that time. The garbage was not buried like it is done today. It was burned in an oil field. This was very dangerous. I remember because the workers would have to wear a harness something like a seeing-eye dog wears. One of the fellows my father worked with fell into the open pit they burned garbage in. It came to a point one time that my father had trouble getting off from work to come and see me so my stepmother would come. She would find out how I was progressing and would report back to my dad. My stepmother and I became very close.

While I was in the hospital, she was the one who taught me the Lord's Prayer. She would bring me books so that I could learn who the Lord was. She knew she would be the one to guide me. I will never forget that she brought me a Bible and told me that I must learn the twenty-third Psalm. Today I say in remembrance to her, because she was the one who compelled me to learn it; this is what guided me through the many years of my hospitalizations.

Some of my experiences with the nurses back in the 1930's were very unpleasant. I feel that the nurses were cruel at times to some of the young patients that were there.

One time my stepmother brought me a nice rubber horse. For some reason I was very fond of horses even as I am today. This particular nurse took my horse away from me and gave it to another boy across the room from me. I guess I went into a rage every time a nurse would come around me. I would either throw the bedpan at them or anything I could get my hands on because I could see the other boy with my little rubber horse that my stepmother gave me. Time passed on and then one day they quarantined me. I was told that I had mumps or measles for over a month and a half. Later, they allowed my stepmother to come. She found out that this was done to punish me for what I had done. I treasured this gift that was given to me.

My stepmother always brought me gifts. She knew I loved hamburgers, so she would stuff them in her bosom, with a coke, wrapped in a towel. With the curtains drawn I would be able to eat the hamburger and soda. She would take the bottle when she left. One time she left a bottle cap on the table. I did not want the nurse to find it. While I was lying in the bed with a cast from my chest to the tip of my toes, I decided that I would hide it. I slipped the coke bottle top down in my cast from my chest and I knew I could work the coke bottle top back up, but it slipped and went down around my side and stayed there. Every time I took a breath, it would be cutting into my side.

The nurse used to check me and soon I was running a high fever and my blood count was going down. The doctors wanted to find out what was affecting my white blood count and why were they being destroyed. To their amazement, they discovered a coke bottle top was embedded to my right side.

After six and a half-years laying on my back in a hospital, the orthopedic doctor who was in charge of my case had a meeting with my stepmother and dad and told them that there was nothing more they could do for me and that it was a good possibility that I would never walk again in life. I had braces on my leg that ran up to my chest. This was very uncomfortable and very hard to walk with. They had made arrangements to send me to Children's Orthopedic Hospital somewhere out in the area called Geddney Farms. I remember so well that my stepmother answered the doctor, "Look, with the help of the Lord, I will prove that you are wrong. George will be able to walk and do what other young boys would like to do in their lifetime." We left the hospital and went home.

After my hospitalization and returning home, I found out that children could be very cruel. I was called crip, gimpy, and other different names. Of course I wanted to give those boys and girls a good shot right in their blowers. With my condition I could never catch them. Later I found out that this was not the right way to approach them. With the help of my stepmother I began to stop being angry at them and wanting to get back at them. I remember one day my stepmother came out from the porch with a bag of marbles. She said "Look here son, here is a bag of marbles, I want you to go out there and show those boys that you can beat them at their game and your father and I will be right beside you." I write this to encourage all disabled children because I really want to help them realize that they can become winners because they have winning capability. The things she taught me at a young age proved right.

My father and I had a strong father and son relationship but more so like two buddies. Many things he knew he taught me, so there were not too many things he knew that I didn't know. He taught me so much in working with tools and equipment.

I side stepped so many holes that I could have fallen into in dealing with people, women, business transactions, and other experiences that I was confronted with. I used to ask him a lot of questions about his youth and growing up. My father smoked cigarettes. If he had a good day of playing poker he would smoke an El Producto, an expensive cigar. He would always go for the best. He told me one day, "Son, in your life you are going to find something that is expensive whether it's a hat, suit or a car. The most expensive one will be the cheapest one you can buy." He told me the truth if it ever was a truth.

When I came home from the hospital my twin sister, encouraged me too. She was always willing to help me and never looked down on me. She gave me self-confidence, and she was a really good student in school. She helped me a lot with my school work. She knew some of the things that I was going through with some of the youngsters in the neighborhood. As I write this book, my sister is still alive and doing well today. She was a leaning rock in some of the hard times I have faced. I love my sister dearly and I write this to her, she has and will always be special to me.

One time my stepmother told me "You have two handicaps against you, but you're going to be able to succeed because you have a good attitude about you and you are a very intelligent boy. Your handicaps are that you are lame in your leg and the other is the color of your skin." My stepmother told me that these two things would haunt me for the rest of my life. She said they were something that would make me so strong I would never have to think about them because I had the intelligence to override them. She told me that was what we were going to work on from there after. She said that she and my father would help me accomplish the things I wanted to accomplish.

Chapter 2

Childhood Lessons

I started out being encouraged by my stepmother and began to gain the proper attitude to deal with children and people because this was very important. I learned so many things about dealing with people and learning to respect adults. When I was a young boy, I never would let my parents hear me say anything that was not proper to an elderly individual even if I did not know them. We were taught to respect all adults no matter what race they were or who they were. I remember one incident.

As a young boy I used to throw stones. I will never forget an Italian man, Mr. Angelo, who managed a little store not far from our house. He was a very dear friend of our family. One day, he saw me throw stones. In those days anyone could correct a child. It was not like it is today. Everyone looked after each other's children. Mr. Angelo caught me and he hollered to me and said, "I saw you throwing stones Georgie, you wait til old Pistol Pete comes home from work. I'm going to tell him Georgie I saw you throwing stones. You are going to be in deep trouble."

I remember begging Mr. Angelo not to tell my dad. I told Mr. Angelo that I did not mean to throw the stones. As I was outside of his store looking around, I told Mr. Angelo that his windows looked kind of soiled. I went in got the bucket, soap and water and started washing his windows in the front. After I finished he said "Gee, you did a real good job. Georgie by the way, sometimes son as you get older you might slip and can't remember things to well."

I think I just about forgot what I was supposed to be telling old Pistol Pete, but look don't you ever let me see you throwing any more stones around here or anywhere else you understand?" I said "Yes sir it will never happen again." This shows how people were in those days. Children respected you. Color didn't mean anything.

One thing we learned was to always respect adults. We would never soil the family name and this I think is forgotten with today's youth. We certainly had morals that we stood for and that your family stood behind.

My stepmother did everything she could to encourage me like any loving mother will do. I remember that she was a great cook. She would make chocolate cakes, coconut cakes and banana cakes. Like any other boy I was fond of food although in those days our parents insisted on us maintaining good eating habits. Even today, I practice good eating habits and I do not overeat. I do not want to gain weight. I believe it would cause more stress on my injured leg and more than likely would be a procuring cause of a decline in my health even more. I really enjoyed her New England style of cooking. My stepmother prepared fish for us every Friday. It seemed to be a religious practice. She would prepare baked beans on Saturdays. I wanted to get really close to my stepmother because to me, she was truly an angel sent from God to help me get through all of the challenges that I had to confront and conquer in my life. I was blessed to have a fairly good singing voice. I remember when I first came from the hospital I would sing a song I learned while I was in the hospital. The title of the song was "In the Valley of The Moon."

(In the valley of the moon)
Down the lane we strolled neath the roses in the valley of the moon
And I lost my love neath the roses in the valley of the moon
We kissed and said goodbye she cried and so did I
Now dear you wonder why I am lonely
But we'll meet again by the roses in the valley of the moon

[fiddle]

Down the lane we strolled neath the roses.

I haven't heard that song in many years now. When I would sing it, my stepmother would just swoon and say "The Lord certainly hasn't forgotten you Georgie, what a wonderful voice you have. I'm sure it will help you along the way in life." She was right because later on it did. During this time, I was in junior high school. I loved music and had a pretty good voice.

During our stay with my father and stepmother, we joined Calvary Baptist Church in our hometown, White Plains, New York. My sister and I were about thirteen or fourteen years old. I remember singing in the choir. I believe in my heart and soul that without the religious background I had my life would have been like a ship without a rudder because where there is no correct guidance, a person will err and may never be able to recover or regain stability for their good, especially when their parents can't help them along life's path.

I know for a fact that there may be times when a parent or parents may be permanently gone and this is just time when our Lord will send someone to help and guide you in the right paths of life. You will have a strong foundation which helps you to discern what right and what is wrong. I feel all children today must first have respect for themselves and of course their parents. A parent can give every boy and girl self-confidence and a positive attitude.

My stepmother used to sit on the front porch and she would crochet or knit a sweater. I remember she could crochet a pocketbook that looked like it was sewn by a machine. She could do it in about three days. She used to knit pocketbooks and this would help bring in income. She would also give them to certain friends. The same with some of the fancy, short sleeve sweaters I used to wear to school. I remember her sitting in her rocking chair, rocking with her slippers on. When I was about fifteen or sixteen years old, I remember one hot summer day, the boys that I played baseball with decided to go down to the Bronx River Park to play ball. I started walking with them to the Bronx River Park. My stepmother saw me walking and she sent my sister to find out where I going. I sent the message back to my stepmother that I didn't know where I was going and I didn't know when I would be back. I recall seeing my sister just running like a deer to deliver the message to my stepmother.

My stepmother came off the porch like a big bear, grabbed me behind the back of the neck and said "Since you don't know where you are going and when you will be back, I am going to send you upstairs to go to bed, and I don't know when I'm going to feed you and I don't know when I'm going to tell you when you are allowed even to get up." This left a mark in my mind that I would never disrespect her or answer her that way again ever in my life. My stepmother was very kind and lovely even though she was firm and didn't allow us to be disrespectful to anyone.

I had a wonderful father too. I think of him from time to time remembering "the good old days." He was a man who had a fifth or sixth grade education. There was something like thirteen or sixteen in his family. He had to leave school to help the family. He had a philosophy of life that I treasure today. He knew so much for a man who had a minimum amount of education but as he said, he had learned a lot from good mothering. He stood for what was right, had a deep respect for all adults, and he would almost die for anything he thought was right. He was a big man, about 240 pounds. Everybody knew him as Pistol Pete. I remember asking my dad how he ended up with a name like Pistol Pete. He said he got that as a young fellow. He and his brothers used to go to dances and one day his uncle, Oscar, shot some guy in the foot who was dancing with his girlfriend. Since all of us looked alike, they blamed me as the culprit and they hung this nickname on me as Pistol Pete.

I used to kid him and tell him that "Gee dad if your skin was white, I believe you would beat old Tom Dewey and you would be the governor of New York State." He puffed his cigar and said "You really think so son?" and I said "You better believe it." I remember him laughing about this incident. On the left side of his face, he bore a scar that ran from his ear down to the corner of his mouth. He told me that he got the scar when he got cut with a knife by a man after leaving a poker game one night. He saw a man beating up a woman and came to her defense. He said that every time the woman got up the man would knock her down again.

One thing I knew was that my dad would fight at the drop of a hat if he saw someone mistreating a child, woman, or an animal. You could be well assured that you would have to deal with him. He told this particular man not to hit this woman again. The woman got up and he hit her again. My dad knocked this guy down and as he went over to her to pick her up, the fellow got up behind him with a knife and cut him from the corner of his mouth to his ear. He said that someone called the police and he was rushed to the hospital and they operated on him. He told me "Son, don't ever get involved with domestic problems and squabbles. Look what I'm carrying on my face." He said after that individual did this, six or nine months later, he saw both of the parties going down the street arm in arm all lovey dovey and here he was left with a scar across his face. Everyone who met him immediately would draw the conclusion that he must be a terrible man.

    He got this scar from fighting but it was in defense of someone that couldn't help herself. He tried to be a Good Samaritan. I asked my dad about my real mother. He told me that she was from Redbank, New Jersey and she was half-Mexican. She was a hairdresser and was a very nice lady. She had the misfortune of passing away after she gave birth to me and my twin sister. When I learned of this news I was somewhat puzzled as to why she died. At that time I didn't understand a lot of things. I just knew I wished she could have been a part of my life to see me and my sister grow up. I am very fond of Latin American music. I remember a few trips I took down to Mexico. I certainly enjoyed it because I knew it was part of my real mother's heritage, although I never had the pleasure of meeting her, at least I know something about her culture. I am somewhat partial to Latin-Americans because their blood flows within my blood too.

Since the polio was slowly leaving me my stepmother took me to an orthopedic store in New York to get special shoes made because my right leg and foot was shorter and smaller than on the left. My stepmother was always on time and I salute her for that quality.

On our way back to Grand Central Station we had to wait for the train. My stepmother went over to a counter to get us something to eat and to drink. She asked me to sit on the bench and wait for her. She went into this little lunch counter and when she got there this lady was cleaning up the counter because a colored woman had just left.

The lady said to my mother, "I just hate waiting on these colored people; it's something about them I really despise. They have a particular odor about them; I can tell them anywhere that I come in contact with them." She said "I sure wish I didn't have to serve them at this lunch counter where I come from we don't have to serve them."

My mother said "Is that right, I wasn't aware that you could tell colored people that way." The lady kept talking and soon the owner of this lunch counter came in. It just so happened she used to be a co-worker of my stepmother. They had worked together at the same garment factory.

My stepmother said to her "Angelia you certainly are hiring some beautiful help these days. This lady here just told me how she really hates serving colored people and that they have a distinct odor about them, and she can tell where ever they were and that she just despises them." Angelia looked at the lady, went over to the cash register and started getting the lady's pay out. She handed it to her and told her she was fired.

The lady told Angelia that "I was talking to this lady here; I didn't say anything to the colored lady." Angelia told her that she had certainly made a deadly mistake because this lady was colored.

At 11 years old, I started school. My mother took me up to Hillside school. When they gave me a test to find out what grade to place me in they found out that I was ready for the fifth grade. I had done well learning in the hospital. I will never forget that they had substitute teachers who would come over to the hospital to teach me mathematics and brought me different books to read; geography and history.

I was fascinated with geography and history books. They seemed to answer questions that I had in my mind of how the world and planets were created and exist.

Since my early childhood days I was always amazed and wondered about creation and how it all functioned. I remember when they told my stepmother they were going to put me in fifth grade. My stepmother told them no and asked them to put me back a year to be sure I wouldn't be struggling to keep up with the other kids. I was put in the fourth grade and performed well. A lady by the name of Mrs. Crawford was my teacher. One of the things all the boys would try to do was sit in the back of the room so they could pass notes and/or talk. One day Mrs. Crawford called me to read something off the board. I struggled reading it. She called me up close to the front of the class and I read the whole thing without missing anything. It was quite obvious I needed glasses. She sent me down to the nurse and I was later sent to an optometrist. I got new glasses. I must have been blind as a bat because when I put those glasses on I never took them off. This was very important to me because many young students believe that what they see everyone else sees the same way. I was failing somewhat in that class because I couldn't see. One thing I did learn that was very important to me was to respect your teacher. Of course at the same time respecting your teacher, they have to earn it too. I know for a fact that teachers have a great impact on their students.

I had several wonderful teachers; Mrs. Crawford, Mrs. Williams from Texas, and the Quaker teachers (a man and woman). They were high school teachers that left a special compelling mark on me. They encouraged me to do the best I could and to be a good student. It is so important for teachers to encourage students, especially if the student is doing exceptionally well in spite of known difficulties or physical ailments. If you can show me a person who has had success in their life; physics, science, electronics or in the business administration field, I can assure you they failed somewhere along the way but did not give up. The thing is that they learned from their failure and were able to pull themselves up by their boot straps and continue on in life. It's no dishonor to fail. I guess in short order there is a saying "tell me and I forget, teach me and I remember, involve me and I learn."

I graduated from the elementary school on Hillside Ave and entered Eastview Junior High School in White Plains, New York. I tried to help my stepmother and father out as much as possible. I was looking for a job at an A&P Store that was on the corner of Hamilton Avenue and Spring Street. I tried so hard to get a job as a box boy. Every attempt I made, they turned me down. I cannot recall how many times that was done to me. One day I came home from school with my report card. I had earned two C's. Back in that day and it's probably still the same, a parent had to sign the report card acknowledging that he or she was aware of their child's grades.

It might also have a note asking the parent to come to the school to talk with the teacher about the subject the child was having problems with. I knew I would be in deep trouble when I gave my report card to my stepmother. After she saw it immediately I had a dish rag wrapped around my head and my mouth. I staggered backwards.

She said, "Let me tell you something son that's why you never got the job at the A&P, do you think they will hire some boy with C's on his report card when they could get another student who has A's?"

She told me "They want winners Georgie and you are going to be one. When I finish going to that high school and meeting with Mr. Miller (who was the principal) and all of your teachers; to find out who is wrong, who is right, and who is a culprit, it better not be you." I knew what that meant. I would not be able to hear the *Lone Ranger, Amos & Andy*, or anything else on the radio. She told me to finish my dinner, finish my homework, and off to bed. My stepmother was strict and meant business when it came down to education. She made sure I completed all of my lessons and made good grades. She never accepted less than my best with school work. We used to have what was called assembly at junior high school on Fridays. I will never forget living in an area with predominately white people. There was something like a hundred whites to every one person of color. The school I attended was predominately white. There were maybe four black students in any classroom. I was sitting in assembly waiting for an individual to come and speak to the students.

I'll never forget as long as I live, that after a few minutes I saw a colored man coming to the stage. I had never expected to see a colored man in our school, especially coming on stage to speak to us. When he began to speak he introduced himself and stated that his name was Mr. Langston Hughes. He was well-known for his poetry. Many people of color and white folks liked him too.

Most of his poetry was written in a southern dialect. He soon discussed his life. He was telling us about how he was in the merchant marines. He caught my interest then because I always loved the sea and ships. I gathered from what he was saying that he went into the merchant marines as a deck hand on a ship named Jeremiah O'Brien. He told us that he had sailed all over the world on different merchant ships. He told us about how he managed during storms and that he had feared for his life several times. He stated that the waves would come in forty and sometimes fifty feet high. They would cover the deck of the ship which made deck hands sailors. He told us of other experiences he had gone through while on these ships going through storms. I was amazed and just kept my eyes on this colored man who was talking to us. He really got me interested because of what he told me personally. He told me that the thing he learned while in the merchant marines was that the radio operator is probably second in command and, at times maybe the most important person on the ship. He said the radio operator tells the captain what information is coming in from other ships, from the coast guard, and what direction to go in order to avoid a storm.

He told me that the captain only knows what the radio operator tells him. I was really impressed with meeting Mr. Langston Hughes and hearing him speak. I never saw him again up close and personal, but I can say that man made a significant impact in my life. I was about 15 years old at that time and it was so inspiring to me to see someone of my own race that had a story about him. I think the name of the book he wrote was *The Big Sea.*

Chapter 3

School Time

One day we were singing in junior high school. Ms. Patti, our music teacher, chose two or three colored students who were in the class to sing Ole Black Joe by ourselves. I wondered why the other children were not singing with us. I guess she wanted us to sing songs from the old south. When I got home I told my stepmother. She looked at me and said "What? I'm to go down to that school to find out why you all have to sing Ole Black Joe without the other students singing it too. Here we are struggling and can't eat in different places in the south and some places in the north. The Urban League and NAACP are fighting in full gear to see that we have the same rights as all other Americans and she wants you three to sing Ole Black Joe. I'll be down to see her." When mother came to the school, she spoke with Ms. Patti. Boy, she dressed that lady down. I felt very bad because Ms. Patti was crying as my stepmother lashed into her. My stepmother told her "There's no way George will sing in that choir. I am going to the principal and the school board to find out why George and a few of his colleagues have to sing "Ole Black Joe" without all members of the choir singing it."

My stepmother felt that it was a song that if sung, we all should sing it. When my stepmother got through with Ms. Patti, that lady changed the whole music schedule. The practice of particular songs that only colored students sang never occurred again.

I remember another incident that happened in school. I guess many folk can recall something that happened at school that was funny and over the years seems even funnier. I still think about what some buddies of mine and I did. Bubie Mills, Bo Jackson, Apple and I were in the same class. We were always together either teasing or rousting one another. We were standing in the hall and this white boy came by and said something to Bo Jackson.

Bo jacked him up by his collar and pinned him against the wall. Bo said "Look fella I'm going to punch you out right here I don't go for that kind of lip service." The boy was in fear for his life.

He said "Don't punch me out whatever you do. I'm sorry I called you kid chocolate, you can call me vanilla." We just burst out laughing and sometimes when we would see one another we would laugh about this incident. For a long time, it was one of the biggest jokes we had on him. While in junior high school word came to the school system that they were offering religious education in a High Presbyterian Church up on Main Street. This was one of the largest churches in White Plains. I was so happy that I was able to sign up for these courses. My prayer today is that they offer religious education for students who want to learn more about our Lord Jesus Christ and the Father of all things God Himself. There were times in my life when if it was not for a strong religious background I certainly wouldn't have been able to accomplish all the things I accomplished or have the trust to get through them. I believe religious education should be available to those who want it and those who don't want it will soon realize what power it gives because it puts wind in your sails when there isn't any wind at all. I tried to stay on the honor roll all the time. **My stepmother was firm on me ever since the incident when I made C's in those classes. She put and indelible data set within my brain "Don't you ever come home with anything less than a B and A is preferred."** She told me if she saw a C her lip would hang down like the tailgate of a truck and it would fall right on the top of my head and I would never forget it. She was right.

I was always involved in singing in the church choir. Rev. Morris was the pastor and the church was on Brookfield Street in White Plains, New York. Our choir usually sang at night and how I enjoyed that so much. Singing in choirs and junior high school helped me because my parents didn't have the money to send me to get vocal lessons. I learned a lot from my teacher in junior high school, Ms. Patti, she taught me to read music which I did quite well. This helped me when I sang in the choir. On Sunday, December 7, 1942, I arrived home around 8:30 pm.

I found out then that we were at war with Japan. During that time I was very good at building things. Anything mechanical whether it was an alarm clock or whatever, I could take it apart and put it back together and it would work. I got interested in electronics too especially radios. I was building a big Taylor aircraft with a 54 inch wing span. You had to have a little motor that you put inside this airplane and it would fly for you. I got this thing three-quarters finished in Japan silk. It was beautiful and here the war had started and I couldn't get any more silk materials. Later during my junior high school years. The wood shop teacher got us involved in aiding the Navy and building identification planes for the Navy, Army and Marine Corp. They needed to be able to identify German and Japanese airplanes so that our personnel in the armed services could identify them as soon as possible. That was really a breakthrough for me to learn about aircraft. I became very good at architectural drawing, topography drawing, and mechanical drawing. All my drawings were in Indian ink. I would say that education then was much better than today. They had a saying where I went to school; you had a better chance of finding teeth in a hen's head than to get an A from Mr. Jennings. I received an A in his class. Because of stepmother encouraging me, I was very positive in thinking. It was at this time that I came face to face with the fact that I did indeed have two handicaps; one I knew was the leg I had polio in, but I found I also had another the color of my skin.

My guidance teacher had a meeting with my stepmother and me. He said "Look, George has a game leg and with the paint job he's got he won't have a chance to use his skills in drawing."

He said "Mrs. Peterson I was looking over his course outline and I see where he's very good in electronics. This is a field I feel that George should go into. The war has just started and they will be looking for men with a strong background in radio and electronics. I pray that you will consider this seriously; maybe later on downstream he'll be able to use some of the things he learned from Mr. Jennings. I see he got an A from Mr. Jennings.

That young man you got there is something else." I felt good about that and I said mom look I'll look more seriously into electronics and maybe that's the way I should go in life.

While I was in high school my dad got ill and was in the hospital for a while. My stepmother had to get a job and work to support our family. He had problems with his kidneys or something. My parents were struggling to make ends meet. My stepmother got a job in the garment industry. She was very good at sewing. It was primarily Italians who worked in the garment district in those days. They taught her how to sew buttons on a shirt and other sewing techniques. My stepmother was always hanging around her Italian friends. If you didn't know what they were saying you could never get a secure job. My mother was fortunate. She spoke Italian fluently. At the same time, they didn't know she was colored because she looked whiter than most of them because her skin was white. Some of them that were olive complexioned were from Sicily. During that time, I looked for a job to help her out. I finally got a job at Mr. Levy's Doll shop. I worked every day after school and a half a day on Saturdays. I wanted to help my family as much as I could.

    I used to pray for snow in the winter because sometimes we'd have snow so deep if you tried to fall down it would support you because it would be right up to your chest. The traffic would be held up all through town. City officials would come to the high school seeking high school students who were willing to work Friday and Saturday and/or half a day Sunday and they would pay. That would really help the family out. I was willing and glad for the opportunity to help my family out more. When my father came home from the hospital we were able to get back on our feet. The little money that I had earned helped support our family and I was very happy that I was able to contribute. We all pitched in and did what we could, my sister included. We all had to help at that time. We were a close knit family and if we ate, we ate together, if we suffered, we suffered together. I'll never forget Ben Patchett, he was

I guess over sixty-five years old when I was only about sixteen or seventeen years old.

He had piercing eyes like two pieces of black coal. He was kind, yet you could see that he had some hard times in his life. He would come all the way from Waycross, Georgia, in the spring to caddy up north where I was caddying. I would listen to him and every time I got the chance to be with him he would take me out to caddy. I learned how to wipe the balls off when they were handed to you with the towel that was on the golf bags. He stressed how important it was to be polite to the people that were playing golf. This was valuable to me because it made the difference as to whether or not you were called upon the next time to caddy. We used to caddy 18-holes. I caddied most times during the spring of the year. It was how I earned money. Back in those days, young people had the capability of getting jobs that are not available today. The attitude of the young people in those days was to respect people whether they were black, white, red, or green and if they were older than you, you respected them. Lord knows I would be in big trouble if my stepmother and father were told by anyone that I had been disrespectful. That would be hell on earth because you'd never live that one down.

At the same time, having a strong religious background was very helpful. Sure there were times that people would get you upset but you learned to bite your tongue. If an adult asked you to help them do this or do that you did it. You did it because you knew your parents standards. You didn't expect to be paid for helping an adult either. You were lucky if they said thank you, which they always did. Your neighbors were acting like your second mother or father. I looked at school teachers the same way; as a second father or mother that could look at a boy or girl and correct him or her. I was talking to Ben one day and he told me about an incident in his life. He said it was right around twenty-nine or thirty when he was coming up north to caddy. Old man John D. Rockefeller used to always play against Harvey Firestone. Firestone was a big time magnate who was buddies with John D. Rockefeller.

All the caddies there knew who were the best players and most of all who were the best payers. At that time it was pretty good if you got two dollars for making a loop around that golf course, and at that time one dollar was like five dollars today. That was big money. I remember as a child that five dollars was like twenty-five dollars. You could buy so many groceries with five bucks that you couldn't carry it all home. This was during the time the depression was well underway. It was hard times. So, Ben got called out to caddy for John D. Rockefeller. Another caddy was called out to caddy for Harvey Firestone. They went around the course of eighteen holes. When the loop was over, Ben said Harvey Firestone gave his caddy two dollars and John D. Rockefeller gave Ben a dollar and one thin dime. For some reason John D. Rockefeller had a habit of taking a dollar and placing one dime in the center of the dollar and folding it up in a strange way. Of course, the caddy that was caddying with Ben teased him about this. Ben got angry. He unfolded the dollar, took the dime out and threw it as far as he could.

It must have been about four or five minutes later that John D. Rockefeller and Harvey Firestone went in and took their showers and came out. Rockefeller called Ben to the front because he wanted to speak to him. So, here comes Ben Patchett from the back of the caddy shop. Rockefeller said "Ben, look". In his hand he had a hundred dollars. When Ben saw it his eyes bucked. Rockefeller said "Look if you give me that dime that I had folded up in that dollar I gave you, which I marked so that I know it when I see it, this hundred dollars is yours."

Ben told me that his heart almost left his body and went straight up into his throat; he said he almost had a heart attack. Ben said he just looked Rockefeller square in the eye, made a 180 degree turn and walked away towards the caddy shop. He said that was a lesson that he never forgot. While I was in high school I was very happy to be able to stay on the honor roll. My stepmother monitored all of my school work.

In June of 1946 I graduated from Eastview High School, formerly Old White Plains High School. In my graduating class were about two thousand white students and about four or five colored students. I'll never forget it. All the students were there in caps and gowns. It was just so wonderful to see these young high school students getting out and going on their way to college or where ever. The school was somewhat of an aristocratic building type. It's been so long since I saw it but I can describe it even now. I hope someday I will be able to go back home to see where I was born and see how things have changed in White Plains and Scarsdale, New York.

Chapter 4

Electronics, Tv's and Radios

After graduation some of my best friends joined the military. Some of them volunteered. I really wanted to serve my country and I felt bad that I was not accepted because of my leg injury. I felt like I was not doing my duty to my country. I loved America and I really would have given my life for this country. Upon them considering me, I was first placed in the 4F category because of my leg. I tried to get into the army anyway by getting in line.

I'll never forget that the doctor who examined me told me "This man's army can't use you in your condition; I am going to have to tell you not to get in this line again." The guy behind me looked at me and said "Look, I'll take your place any day." He never knew my feelings. I was thinking that if I was able to go and did not get killed in battle, I would be able to get a college education and other benefits after the war. I was thinking of serving and being served an education. I remember telling my mom and dad about it. They didn't know but something stayed with me that I never forgot from the assembly we had in junior high school with Mr. Langston Hughes.

I remembered that Mr. Hughes spoke to us about the power that a radio operator had aboard a ship. This really sunk in my head and left a mark on me. Afterward I became interested in the Morse code and how radios worked, building them from kits, and other sorts of things. From what Mr. Hughes told us, the thing I remembered most was that a radio operator on board ship is almost as important as the captain especially during a battle or a storm. He told us that the captain only knew where they were going or what the circumstances were from the radio operator.

The captain knew something about the radio room but didn't know how to send Morse code, nor the correct manner. I began thinking of joining the merchant marines like Langston Hughes did. I had a friend, James Pees, in junior high school who had an ear problem and the military wouldn't accept him either. He went into the merchant marines. He used to tell me stories about how he sailed around Russia, India, and to Johannesburg, South Africa.

He told me a story of something that happened in Johannesburg, South Africa. He said because he was black and not accepted by Africans in Johannesburg, white people in Johannesburg just ran him back on the ship. He told me that he just stayed on the ship swept the decks, cleaned up other areas on board ship, and checked all the equipment on the ship until they got loaded and ready to sail again. A buddy of mine had gotten out of the Navy and bought a nice, used 1951 Cadillac. He worked for IBM and he wanted me to try to get a job at IBM too. He wanted us to work together but I had my eyes set on other things. I remember him driving back and forth to Poughkeepsie, New York averaging about twenty-one miles to the gallon. I think he paid $1400 dollars for the car. I had bought three automobiles and my buddy was still riding in the same car saving money. I guess my dad was right about buying the best. My buddy would wear a Brooks Brothers suit, Stetson hat and Florsheim shoes. When he died, these items went in the grave with him. I remember him telling me one time that when you put on a Brooks Brothers suit and a Stetson hat rain would just roll off of it.

I used to kid him and say tell me something about your life when you were young. He told me, "Oh yeah, we used to have a thing when I was a child that when we met another colored boy who moved into our neighborhood we would walk up to him and say here's a penny, the boy would say what's this for and we would say I swore if I met a guy that was blacker than me I would give him a penny, and boy the fight would start right then."

He said when the dust cleared away, they would buy a bottle of root beer and they all would sip off the same bottle of root beer as the sign of their friendship. They were friends until the very end of their lives. I wish sometimes that life was that way today.

The things my dad had a great weakness for was not poker or skin games even though he loved them. It was baseball, the fights, and boxing. I guess I'm more of a fight fan myself. In those days we only had the old GE radio. I'll never forget when the radio broke down. My dad was quite upset that it had to break down just when the ball game was going to be starting the next day or something like that. So, he said son take this up to the radio store and get it fixed for me will you and I said sure I'll take it up there. I walked up to Hamilton Avenue to the old Greyhound bus station where there was a radio store owned by a man called Mr. Hielderman. They called him Major Hielderman. He used to be in the military in the early days of the exhibition force that was up in Iceland. He was in communications and a heck of a great guy. That man really helped mold my life to what it is today. I learned so much from him. Anyway, when I brought the radio in and put it on the counter, he said "I told you this thing is just making a racket and that you can't hear anything on it just a loud hum and whatnot."

He looked me square in the eye and told me "I'm not fixing this radio for old Pistol Pete any more, from here on in you're gonna be fixing radios yourself. Come on in the back with me; let me show you what's wrong with it."

He took me in the back and showed me that it was the output filter or something on it that had lost its composites and wasn't filtering the DC through the radio, and that caused the humming. He said we'd pull the filter composite out. He let me use his tools to put the compasser in and he taught me how to solder. That was a giant step for me to learn and I was happy he involved me. He had opened a door for me to something that would follow me for the rest of my life. It seemed that I couldn't get away from it. This man really is the one who started me in taking steps into the field of radio, electronics, and communications.

I wanted to go to electronic school especially after Mr. Hielderman showed me how valuable this would be for me. I looked into getting in to school but of course it took money. My family was poor and my dad only earned twenty-five dollars a week. He had a wife and two children that depended on him. He really had a lot on his hands. He was such a great guy. He was willing to work more to pay for my education after I graduated but I told him no. I tried to be independent and on my own. I told him that if he could pay the $11.25 for my train ticket on New York Central, I'd do the rest myself. So between me caddying, helping people move things, and carrying packages for women to their apartments I was able to earn a few dollars. It dawned on me that I should try out for some of the amateur hours. Maybe I'd get a chance to get a few dollars to go to school. I tried at a few of the nightclubs in New York City and Harlem, and many other places trying to get money for school.

 Finally, I signed up for the Apollo Theatre. I will never forget the day when they came to take me to the Apollo Theatre. I went down on the train. I remember my cousin saying; yeah I know you're going to do well. His real name is Arthur Pallor but we called him Sonny boy. He said you know I'll be rooting for you and I said you bet I'll try to do the best I can.

Singing at the Apollo was really an honor for me. I sang a song titled "You Go to My Head" by Freddie Coots. It was something that all the great colored singers, Ella Fitzgerald, Billy Eckstein, and Arthur Prysock had to get acceptance and approval from the Apollo. If you didn't pass that test, you wouldn't pass any other test. When you went to sing you were expected to perform your best. You could not come on stage to just clown around because the people would get angry at you if you did. If you didn't have what it took to be a winner, the people knew it and would "boo" you off the stage. If you kept on performing anyway, the crowd would get furious and actually start throwing things at you and even come up on the stage and throw you right off. There was a guy behind stage who would then come out to escort you off the stage with some sort of joking dance or moves. I believe he was called Puerto Rico. The people attending came to be entertained and you'd better do it or else. I was fortunate to be chosen as the first prize winner. I received $25 and a contract from the orchestra that played for me. There was a gentleman by the name of Sid Oliver. He wanted me to be his vocalist.

I brought the contract home with me for my stepmother and father to read. I wanted to be successful. I would be traveling with the band. I'll never forget my stepmother sitting down and talking to me and saying Georgie, I talked to your father and we feel that it is not wise for you to travel over the road singing. She told me that they wanted me to keep singing in the church choir and for occasions that would help people like weddings, funerals or whatever. She said please hear me Georgie and don't get into this.

She reminded me of what happened to my friend Jimmy Regell. He was a buddy of mine that was in the first airborne. He had also won singing at the Apollo. He had a very nice voice, and he was artistic. He could draw like Michelangelo. I remember one time he told me he hit someone with a brick during a fight. He ended up in jail. He told me that he drew the Lord's Prayer with charcoal on the walls where he was incarcerated.

The commanding officer thought he was so good at drawing that he released Jimmy from jail. It was coming up to Christmas. He got out of jail and sang the rest of his time in the first airborne for the commanding officer and others. After a while he started drinking, fooling around with women, went into a tail spin and never came out and finally it killed him. My stepmother didn't want that to happen to me. I guess she could see maybe me going down that same path if I had chosen to travel over the road with those guys. Thanks to her and the dear Lord, I focused my interest on my education. I decided to take the $25 and go to an electronic school and that is what I did.

I enrolled with **Delehanty Institute** and graduated. There were times I didn't know how I was going to get through the day. I struggled many times to get money to pay for my education. I remember the Director of the school telling me one time not to worry about the debt because he had faith in me. He said, "I know you'll pay George because you're that type of boy." Praise the Lord that I was able to go to school. On my last day of school I gave the Director the final payment I owed to Delehanty Institute. When you're raised the right way it enables you to succeed and accomplish things that are almost unbelievable.

After I graduated from Delehanty Institute, I enrolled in an advanced class at **Philco Advance Television Course** on Hunters

Point, Long Island, New York. I gained more knowledge and experience repairing different television models, especially color televisions. They were just becoming available at that time. When I finished school at Philco, I went back home and was hired to work at a company named Transvision Television Corporation on Lexington Avenue. The store was across the street from the Studebaker Shop which had been there for many years. I went in and spoke with a man by the name of **Johnny Myer,** who would become my boss. He was the manager of the television repair shop. I began work putting up antennas and repairing different television models. The Transvision Television Corporation became well known for its television that came in a kit.

  The consumer could put it together up to tubes sizes of 12 inches. They were selling very well in that area. Sometimes people had problems fixing them and would bring them back to the shop. I performed all repairs.

  One day as I working, the Joe Louis fight was about to start. A man came into the shop to have his television repaired. He asked me if I could I fix it for him. I said by all means. It was getting dark and I was getting ready to close the shop. I told him I didn't want to stay too late. I wanted to get home to check on stepmother.

I took his television and began to inspect it to find out the problem. Before long, I had fixed his television. When I got through fixing it he proceeded to take his television and put it in his car.

I said "Wait a minute here, you owe me **forty-five dollars.** " He said "Look I am the owner of Transvision Television Corporation. I'll talk to John Myer tomorrow and get it all squared away with him." I told him "That's fine that you talk to John Myer tomorrow but you pay me today or I'll make sure that you're up in that jail cell on Martin Avenue, that's where the jail is located if you don't know. " I said "If not, leave the television here and when you come tomorrow to talk to Johnny you can pick it up then." The gentleman got irritated. He went in his pocket, pulled out forty-five dollars and paid me for the repair service that I had done on his television. I told him to have a nice evening and enjoy the fight. Well, lo and behold that man came back the next day. I looked out of a window and saw him talking to John Myer, my boss. When Mr. Myer came back into the store, he said "Well George; it looks like you're in charge of the shop now. That was the boss you were dealing with last night. He seems to like what you were doing here, and he put you in charge of the whole Transvision Shop."

He said "I'll be working outside in the Portchester and Greenwich, Connecticut area." He told me that he would be checking in on me from time to time to make sure everything was alright with me.

I was shocked to learn that the man I had demanded payment from was the owner of the Transvision Corporation. I had jammed him real good. It didn't make any difference to me. I was on a job and handling business. Business is business. I stayed with Johnny Myer and the Transvision Corporation for about or three years.

Chapter 5

Learning from the Best

The war was still going on. I felt that I wasn't doing my part in helping the soldiers and sailors who were fighting. I felt I had to do something for the war effort because all of my friends were going into the armed services. I felt sort of out of it by not being able to go into the service like the other young men were. I had tried a few times to enlist in the army and the navy. I loved the navy best of two. I was told by one of the recruiters that they didn't want me because of the condition with my leg. I was told to just stay home and wait this thing out. I was disappointed and just couldn't stand it. I found out there was an opening over at a company in Elmsford, New York, called the **Sonatone Corporation.** They were making small tubes that were used primarily in radar equipment and high tech transmitters for aircraft. I was hired and worked as an Industrial Electronic Technician. I got all kinds of praises from a gentleman by the name of Cliff Van Tassel. He seemed to be a great guy. I worked there for about one year. I noticed that a lot of the men were being laid off.

I was wondering why and saddened to hear of their job loss. I knew they had families who were depending on their income. Some of the guys were crying as they would leave the place. They knew it would cause more stress and strain for their families. I felt very bad about it. I'd rather get laid off myself than see them go like that, although it would be hard for me too.

I was single and lived at home with my father and stepmother. My dad was in the hospital at the time and I was helping my stepmother the best I could. I was wondering why they were being laid off and I was not. I was told by my boss, "Oh no with the job you're doing you won't have any problem, they would have to close down this whole place before they ever laid you off. "

I took him at his word. I had an old 1951 Chevrolet and although it was still running I decided to get a new one.

All my family was dealing with General Motors at that time and I knew the people down at the Chevy dealer. I went down there and bought a 1954 Chevrolet on Thursday. On Friday when we got paid I got a pink slip along with my check and I was really shocked. I didn't know what was going on. I learned from that, and maybe other people can learn too, you only have yourself to bank on.

There's no one that can keep you on any job. I went back home and told my mom and dad about it. I received a little severance pay and decided to go deer hunting up near Albany, New York. I used to going hunting up there with my friends. I thought Lord today, it is really something else to realize; here I have a brand new car and not job the first, but jobs in my field were quite plentiful.

So, when I came back from deer hunting I said I'd just settle in. There was a company named General Precision in Pleasantville, New York. I decided I would go there and see what they had. I felt sure I could get a job there and lo and behold I did. I got a job working with the final output of the country's testing of our design of APN81. They were making a guided missiles system for the Navy. I was right in the last check up on these guided missiles systems with all their gyroscopes and whatnot. After we checked them out they went to the Navy.

It wound up later that I got interested in another company. It was the Nevis Cyclotron Laboratory on the Hudson River. It was very close to Yonkers and Terry Town. I went out there to seek a job. The Nevis Cyclotron Laboratory was run by the Atomic Energy

Commission (AEC) lead by Dr. James Rainwater, the Nobel Prize winner for the atomic bomb.

He had worked with Dr. Upperhinder in White Sands New Mexico. When I got there, I filled the paperwork out. The gentleman that was sort of second in command that was actually getting the help for Dr. Rainwater, took me to where Dr. Rainwater was. It was my understanding from him that Dr. Rainwater had about six or eight nuclear submarine technicians. He said they stayed something like a month, at most five or six, and they were out of there. I said is that right. He said I think you can only last about five days. I said five days. He said no three days and you're going to be out of here too. He said because I don't think you're going to be able to hack it with **Dr. Rainwater**.

I said well I guess we'll just have to see won't we. As we passed a desk, there was a gentlemen sitting there with his feet upon the table looking at quota mechanic figures. He was changing each perimeter calculating to see what the results were from what I could gather. He didn't even introduce me to him. He didn't say anything to me and I didn't say anything to him. He had jeans on, nice walking shoes, nice shirt and whatnot and he got up and began writing some mathematics on the blackboard which I recognized as quota mechanics and I looked at it. I was there for some time so I put my lunch down. I wasn't going to disturb him. I sat down and watched him as he changed one of the numbers which was in his problem to see what the variance would do to create this or that. After a while, I got up off the chair and went over to the file and pulled it out to see what they had here. They had an old 108 channel unit little computer that they were using. It was used to check the pulses that were coming from this magnetron that was a slow neutron spectrometer group which is really high on the list with our government for developing the shielding for nuclear submarines and things of this sort; battle wagons and aircraft carriers. I was looking around down there and they had this maybe 350 syn-cyclotron which was used in the Hudson River to suck water in to cool down the big magnets in there. It's very hot.

I went around looking in the drawers going over all the paperwork and walking all over to see what they had there. I was shocked that they were not well organized.

I thought that they would really be state-of-the-art. And so I looked on. They had tubes that were facing the wall and fans were blowing to cool them down, but the chassis was open facing our room. Dr. Rainwater could change the components to make the pulse sharper, wider, or whatever he wanted to do. They had two or three scopes 545's, 535's and different equipment to check what was going on in the electronic area of the chassis they had on the racks in front of us. It was close to 4:00 p.m. by the time I got through reading all the stuff, seeing what the guy had, and taking notes. He had been watching me and I was aware of this of course. I was going through paperwork and getting up to speed. It was around 4:30 pm now and this gentleman was still changing variables and working quota mechanics problems on the black board. So, I started to get some of my things together to go home. He walked over to me and said "I understand that you are the new Nuclear Research Technician here in our laboratory. I said yes sir I am. He said well I'm Dr. Rainwater. I said oh, well I'm delighted to meet you sir and it's a deep honor. He said I like what you're doing, carry on; I think you might fit in here with us just fine. I said thank you sir and that's how we met. He and I just locked up like that. I was his main man thereafter. He knew he had someone who did not need anyone to hold their hand and tell them what to do. I surely enjoyed working with him. The things I learned from him were just unbelievable. We would have to go about eight stories down to the ground where they had this cyclotron.

You could open the window there and the electronic neutrons would fly out. We had sample changes so that we could control the different materials we were using. For targets we would go out to a target shack where I would set up all the Corenkuff detectors and things out there to accept certain particles when we put a certain sample there like rare earth, gold or silver. One time we had close to sixty-five pounds of pure gold from the Mint of Philadelphia.

I'll never forget when they came; they had guards standing around with machine guns while they were delivering it to us. They would cut samples and put it in sample change to see what neutron particles were absorbed and what it did not absorb. The particles that we were testing, primarily the neutrons because they were deadly, were the highest quality of radiation that one can have, more potent than radiate itself. It was such a great honor to learn all this stuff. It was told to me that Dr. Rainwater worked steadily when there was a problem or something he couldn't figure out. He would stay two or three days just constantly working on that thing. In fact,

I was told that one time he worked so long that he didn't cash his checks. It sort of screwed the bank up with getting their accounting squared away. I started chuckling over that because I said this man is really dedicated. At the same time I got more and more involved and interested in nuclear research. One day we were going pretty smooth for quite a while and all of a sudden the equipment came to a stop. Dr. Rainwater came in from the old 535 and the 545 scope in the lab to see why the sudden pulse had stopped.

Time was money and we were losing valuable information. We were bombarding a special a material eight floors down below in our sample changer to see what signals it would absorb. We were working with the Navy and the AEC in order to ensure the safety of all personnel working on the nuclear submarines and aircraft carriers that we would be building.

It was also our task to work in conjunction with the Navy to get this information in to protect all our personnel on board these large submarines and aircraft carriers. Dr. Rainwater was working on this project and now it just didn't seem to want to work at all. He began to work at finding out why everything had suddenly come to a halt. I was changing components with him, changing this and changing that. I thought, well let me go in the back end and look around because this thing is all tubes. It wasn't solid state. I looked back there and lo and behold there was a 6AH6 store vacuum tube that was just cold dead. No filament at all in it. I said I've got to let him know that we can put the tube in it and get it running because I'd like to see what's happening too.

I guess I was just as excited about what we were doing as he was. I thought how do I tell this gentleman that if we change this tube we can get this show on the road? Here is the man that won the Nobel Prize and confirmed that the atomic bomb worked. I finally said excuse me Dr. Rainwater, I don't know if this is of any value to you in what we are doing here, but it appears to me that there's a 6AH6 with filaments that aren't lit. It looks like it's in the same area that you're working in. He looked back behind the chassis and he could see it.

He looked in my eyes and said O.K. Peterson; I need to take a break anyway. Change everything back the way it was and put a new tube in there. I'll be back in about an hour and a half. I'm going to get a bite to eat and I'll get the show on the road. He said thanks a million take care; it's all in your hands. I said sir yes and that's what I did. I knew that you had to know how to handle these particular men, what to say and how to say it. Lord knows he was giving me an education there. I considered it a deep honor to have worked with all the fine gentlemen at Nevis in the development of shielding for all our submarines and aircraft carriers.

I really appreciate Dr. Rainwater giving me a chance when no one else gave me a chance. I would ask him questions and he would explain things to me. He trusted me deeply and I trusted him. What a fine gentleman he was. I know the man that took me down to meet Dr. Rainwater thought I would only last three days. He was judging me by the color of my skin instead of the content of my character and what I had under my hat. The Columbia University Physics Department was also a partner in the Nevis Cyclotron Laboratory. I helped four graduate students to get their masters degrees and my name was mentioned in five doctor's theses. Dr. Rosen worked in our lab, George Grimm and Bill Frati came from Brookhaven on Long Island, and Scott Desjardins was from Brown University, I helped them all to get their doctorates. They mentioned me for helping them because when they fell asleep on their experiments I would run the whole thing for them.

I met some wonderful men from China, India, and all around the world. They were really great guys. I loved them all, yet Dr. Rainwater was the main man. He and I were very tight.

Dr. Rainwater was thin, about 185 pounds, well built, had high cheek bones and walked on the tip of his toes. He was sharp and I loved that about him. When he would go down the stairs he would usually duck because there was a steel bar across the steps and he didn't want to bump his head on it. One day as he was going his way, I was getting things all squared away because we were starting our experiment again. Lo and behold I heard this boom, I ran out to see what had happened and saw that Dr. Rainwater had hit his head on that steel bar. He was weaving as if he was getting ready to fall straight down the stairs. It looked like the hit had stunned him. It appeared he didn't know whether to go backwards or straight down the stairs. I ran to him, grabbed him under both arms and dragged him back from the stairs to keep him from falling down the stairs. I said Dr. Rainwater are you okay?

He looked at me with his dark piercing eyes, they looked like laser beams penetrating coal, and he said yes I am Peterson. He said you know that's the great tragedy of man's anatomy. If I had a twenty-seven degree sloping forehead like the rabbit I would have seen that steel bar up there. As I watched him, it looked like a big navel orange began to grow out of the side of his head where he had hit it. I asked him did he want to put something on it because it didn't look too good. He said oh that's alright Peterson. I wish to thank you for what you did for me.

I said oh it's an honor to do for you or anyone else. He said carry on with what you were doing and he went down the stairs and was gone. He helped me in so many ways. I don't think he knew how much he was doing for me but Lord knows there was nothing that I wouldn't do for him. We had a certain time that the cyclotron was ours. We usually had a two to three week time limit to do our experiments.

Sometimes we worked three weeks straight night and day, but I hung in there with him. I worked the early morning shift from 8:00am – 4:30pm. It was certainly very warm in there because they always had the tubes turned towards the wall where the fans were blowing and the windows open to blow the heat out. **The cyclotron was a hot tamale. It was a 350 MVP syn-cyclotron. It was cooled down by the Hudson River which would suck the water in and cool** this thing down. There were giant magnets in there. When you went near it you had to be very careful and be sure not to wear anything metal or oh my Lord, it would tear keys right out of your pocket. I met some of the top nuclear physicists from all over the world who came to see what we were doing. Nuclear research engineers and physicists are different from regular electrical engineers. They have broad knowledge in all the fields that they work in whether its mechanics, electronics or nuclear physics itself. They can come up with ideas and things to do that I call Yankee engineering, which I've been doing all my life. My mind is sort of programmed in that direction. I did that beforehand; pulling alarm clocks apart and fixing them for senior citizens, and fixing radios and things.

I didn't care what it was; I'd fix it and make it run. I went to electronic schools all over New York. I know of three young fellows who died at Nevis while trying to take short cuts. They thought that they could jump the magnetron there in the cyclotron. They would use jumper cables so they could take a short cut. I never did that because I knew that was very dangerous. I had read about the nuclear physicists in Los Alamos. They noticed that there was something happening within their cyclotron. One of them went in there and pulled the two materials apart that were lock together. He reached in and pulled them a part physically with his hands. That of course was signing his death warrant and he died from that radiation later on. In that area also, we had dosimeters that we clipped on our shirts or jacket. Every month they would pick them up and take them down to the laboratory. They would check them to find out whether you had been in a strong radioactive environment.

They would send you down to Columbia University in New York in a special van to have you checked out down there. I tried to be careful. They used to kid me all the time because I was always gun shy. I didn't like fooling around with that stuff. I saw a rat one day walking around in the cyclotron. I could see big knots on him that were leaking puss or something out of them. It scared the daylights out of me. I thought about what it could do to a human being. He looked like he was intoxicated, staggering around and highly radioactive. I became more cautious in knowing where I was working.

Chapter 6

God is Always with Me

Time went on. We worked more experiments. We knew that we had to get more resolution for us to check our pulses. In that way we would know exactly how many particles were getting into the materials that we put into the sample changes. We wanted to see the protective cell that sits on our submarines and aircraft carriers. We had a 37 meter flight path, where I went out and set up all the Corenkuff detectors with oscilloscope and checked them out with a radium sort. I set them out where at certain levels they would cut off, so that we could see the particles and were aware of what particles were getting through and what particles were not. We could set the gating system on our Corenkuff detectors and things of that sort. I remember Dr. Rainwater said we were going to have to change our flight path. Instead of 37 meters we were going out 100 meters. I said yes sir, and that's what we did. It was somewhere close to the end of June and getting very hot. I took my jacket off with my dosimeter on it, and laid it very close to Dr. Rainwater's desk. I worked out in the field getting all our equipment into that

100 meter shack. We were setting up all our equipment to be able to check the flight path of the neutron particles that would be used.

We wanted to see how they actually were being absorbed on certain materials that we were using in the cyclotronic sample change. We were using nuclear research equipment so that the Corenkuff detector would be set off by radium and things of that sort. We had a lead ball that looked like a large softball. The top came off and we would use a long stick to lift it up and put radium under there.

We would then set the levels on our Corenkuff detector depending on what kind of materials we were using. We were using gold, silver and all kinds of materials to see what would protect our sailors on board our ships. At that time, I said well gee I'll make sure everything is squared away here in this shack and Dr. Rainwater said hey Peterson, it looks like you're kind of interested in bows and arrows. I said oh yeah; all my life, my grandfather taught me. He was part of the Iroquois tribe and was raised in York, Pennsylvania. I told him he used to take me to make homemade bows from over the stone wall we had next to our six acre farm. My grandfather loved bow hunting. That's how I got interested in bow hunting deer.

Bow hunting became my heart, I really loved that. And he said that's great, wonderful, maybe we can set you out a little shooting range after a while. I said well that would be great Dr. Rainwater but I want to get this underway so we can started up. I'm very interested in seeing the results of what's going to happen here. One day I got a phone call from Dr. Rainwater after my dosimeter had been checked. He said I noticed Peterson that you have been around a hot pile. I said no I don't remember that, I'm the one that's really gun shy. Dr. Rainwater said well you can't be too careful, but we go by what we see here. Your white blood cells are being destroyed. I said what am I going to do? I knew I had made sure I was protected when they lifted the top off that radium sort which was the size of a large softball. I did the same when we moved it under our Corenkuff detectors.

Then I would set them up to the level that Dr. Rainwater wanted them set for the experiments. Now they were saying I had been over exposed.

Dr. Rainwater said your dosimeter shows you've been around a very hot pile, and I started sweating. He said they are going to send a van up here to take you down to St. Luke's at Columbia

University to check you out. They checked me out. They didn't notice anything as far as my blood. Everything was all right. They told me that my dosimeter reading was showing that I had been around a very hot pile. I said oh boy I wonder what's happening to me. They said the dosimeter doesn't lie. They asked me where did I work, what had I being doing and several other questions. I said gee I don't understand how this could happen. Dr. Rainwater said that when neutron beams hit this, it just sets this thing on fire. He asked me I bet you glow in the dark don't you? I said I don't know. I was not aware of that. By this time I was married to my first wife Gloria and we had two children. I said my wife didn't tell me she could see me in the dark, and I said I'll certainly be careful. He said yeah, we're going to have to have you come back again. I was really concerned after that. I didn't say anything to my wife about it. I did check my insurance to see how that was. We had another week or so to get ready for our experiments to start kicking off. We ran two to three weeks a month with our experiments and we were just finishing the one with the shack. Anyway, it happened that one day while I was working I got very sick and I said Lord what's wrong with me.

I went into the restroom to use the urinal and I felt kind of funny, dizzy like. I almost fell on the floor into the urinal. I called the office upstairs to let Dr. Rainwater and Dr. Rosen know that I was sick and needed to go home. I went down the steps carefully so I wouldn't fall on them, got to my car and started driving home. I was wondering the whole time if the dosimeter was telling the truth. I was weaving all over the highway. I know that if a highway patrolman had seen me going home he probably would have locked me up. He would have thought that I had been drinking and given me a ticket for DUI or something. I got home and when I got there my wife said look, you had better go to the hospital to find out what's wrong with you; you don't look right to me. She took me to the hospital. I was still sort of staggering.

There was a Dr. Neiger there at White Plains hospital. He checked me out and called two attendants and told them to get a stretcher. He said we have to take him up right now for an operation. I almost died right there. I said what do you mean an operation. He said something is certainly wrong. It looks like appendicitis in the worst way and we must operate immediately. Your blood count is going crazy. I said oh Lord those people were right. I guess I have been around a very hot pile because all my white blood cells are being destroyed. That's a sign that you have been around a hot nuclear pile. I said Lord here I go. They called Dr. Rainwater and others and told them that I was being operated on and that I would be out of work for a week or so.

I was admitted and for the next two hours I was on the operating table being operated on for appendicitis. In fact, after they took my appendix out it burst in Dr. Neiger's hand. He told me the Lord has certainly been with you George because when I took your appendix out it burst in my hand. I told him I will always be indebted to you sir. He said you would not have never been here and I would not have been telling you this if it had burst in you; you would have been a dead man. He said I'm so happy we took care of this. I told him you saved my life.

I learned that with appendicitis, the white blood cells can be destroyed the same as if you were in a hot nuclear field or around a pile of radium. While I was in the hospital it turned out that they found something out about the jacket that I had been wearing. Dr. Rainwater was doing some experiments downstairs away from his office and he had this radium sort up there with the top off under some papers. Since it was buried under the papers no one saw it. It was right next to my jacket and caused the dosimeter to just go crazy. I guess if I had been working near his desk, instead of changing another flight path for a beam that was coming and striking our target, I probably would be a dead man today. But the Lord was with me again as always. They told me about the entire incident after they had found the error. This is something I'll never forget. I thought it to be a sign from the Lord telling me that I should be getting my hat and scooting out of there. Three men had already died there.

When I got back on my feet again I was hesitant to go to the lab. I was really gun shy of everything I was doing or anything someone else was doing around me because it was a very hazardous job. We were always given a **month of vacation.** I often wondered was that to let us get away from the hot stuff that we were working with. I had a brother-in-law that lived in Albuquerque, New Mexico. He wanted us to come out and visit him. I thought this was a great chance to go west. I had never been west but always wanted to go. My mother-in-law kept our children and Gloria and I were on our way. My brother-in-law was a photographic technician in the Air

Force. He told me about a nuclear physicist he had met and said maybe you'd like to go to work in their laboratory. That was where the atomic bomb was actually developed with Dr. Rainwater. It was down in White sands which I think was about 300 or 400 miles south of Albuquerque, New Mexico. We made the trip there and my brother-in-law introduced us to the gentleman. He and his wife invited us to have dinner with them. He looked very interesting. I guess my brother-in-law had told him about me because he wanted me to go to work for him right then. My brother-in-law was aware that I was looking for a change in my work or something new. The gentleman knew about Dr. Rainwater and had talked with Dr. Rainwater about me. While we were having dinner with this nuclear physicist and his wife, Gloria asked his wife what she didn't like about that living area. She said one of the things she didn't like was that they had to chain the garbage cans up because black bears would come down and flip them over. Garbage would be all over the place. She said the bears would turn the garbage cans over like they were little cans of soup or something. The physicist said dogs would start barking and they would know the bears were out there. When the bears got tired they would just move away.

Boy that wife of mine, at that time said, "You're not working here. I don't want to have to deal with something like that George; looking at five to six hundred pounds with teeth an inch and a half long and claws that would tear you to pieces." She said no, you will not be working out here, that's out.

I said, "Is that right?"

And she said, "Yes."

So I said, "Well, I'm not going to work there."

We crossed the United States in our car, just Gloria and I. The children stayed with their grandmother back in Portchester, New York.

I told Gloria, "Alright look, we've come this far, we're three quarters across the United States. I'm going to see Aunt Virginia in Pasadena, California and put my feet in the Pacific Ocean."

I wanted to see what was on the coast and at least say I had been there. I also wanted very much to see Aunt Virginia. She was a lovely lady and I thought highly of her. She was my mother-in-law's best friend. They were from Pittsburgh, Pennsylvania. She had moved to Pasadena, California to be with her son who was working for the Navy.

His job in the Navy was loading ammunition on ships. Someone dropped one of the bombs they were loading onto the ship. The whole ship blew up and he was killed. I loved that lady and she loved me. She took to me as if I was her son. We would laugh a lot. She was like my second mother. While we were there visiting Aunt Virginia, Gloria wanted to go shopping. I said, "well I'll let you all be together and I'm going to make a stop at UCLA."

I went to the UCLA Laboratory to look at their Van digraph machine. I was told that they had one over there. I wanted to see what it looked like and see if it was similar to what we had at Columbia University. I got there and checked it out. Then I got to talking with people asking questions about their diffusion pumps, kennie pumps, and corenkuff detectors. I asked them what computers they were using to analyze the data they received and so forth. They were using a different technique from what we had at Columbia University with Dr. **Rainwater**. They said you've worked in an atomic energy field. I said a little bit. They said no not a little bit or you wouldn't be asking all these questions.

I gave them my resume and told them I worked with Dr. Rainwater at Columbia University on the Manhattan project developing shielding for battle ships, submarines, giant carriers and shielding personnel. They said Rainwater was an alumnus of UCLA and I said yes I understand that, he's a fine man and I think the world of him. I don't know if I'll ever get another boss like him. I told them that I learned so much from Dr. Rainwater.

The man in charge asked me why I was planning to resign from Columbia University. I said it was time for me to shift gears and step into other branches of the scientific field. I told him the atomic energy field was fine but I had wound up having a problem. He asked what it was. I told him I'd started to glow and now my wife could see me in the dark. He looked at me and laughed and said oh I understand what you are saying. He asked me what I knew about video. I told him I paid my way through electronic school fixing big RCA 630 chassis. He told me that there was a project going on now at Devil Gate Canyon in the Jet Propulsion Laboratory which is run by NASA. It was a secret place and it was back in the mountains. He said they had laboratories and special things going on there. He thought I would be a good candidate because I had top secret clearance having worked with Rainwater and I was heavy into video. He said they had been looking for someone like me. He asked me what I was doing that day. I said I was just checking with you guys to see what new thing was happening in the world of data processing. He said I'd like you to go over and talk to some people there. I said is that right. He said yes I think you would fit in very well over there. I thought to myself that this would be a good opportunity for me to go over and get a look at where it was at and what was going on. I went out there. I didn't know it but they made a phone call and set up an interview for me for that day. I had to go through a big tall gate with Marine guards on each side with automatic rifles and machine guns protecting it at all times.

When I walked into their laboratory it was really together and the set up was very professional. They were waiting at that time for a gentleman to come in.

They began to review my résumé'. One person said it's hard for me to believe you have already gotten your name on four doctor's thesis in nuclear physics. He said you were there with them six years? I said yes I was there with them night and day. I told him that I gave up everything to help our nation and those fellows laboring for their doctorates. I said you guys know my second boss,

Fred Billingsley from Birmingham, Alabama, he's a great guy. I think the world of him and his family. He said yes we're planning to have him work with us because he's heavy into video and we need that for the projects that we'll be working on for NASA. He told me that The Ranger would be coming in the next four to six months. He said we need someone with your background as well, but first you have to meet the head of our facilities here at the Jet Propulsion Lab. He said I also want you to meet the director of our high tech color image processing lab. He will be here shortly. He's the man that says yea or nay. I said that's great. I waited a while and here comes this gentleman. When he came in they said hello Mr. Arcan, this is the man who is interested in what we are doing and would like to work in our laboratory. When he walked up closer, I looked and saw who he was. I said hi Artie how are you doing. He said well I'll be dog gone, what are you doing here?

I said it looks like they might want to hire me. He said it'll be good to have you on board with us. I said you know I'll give it my best Artie. Artie said all the good old boys are here; Chuck Tiger, the engineer you used to work with, is here. I think you'll like it here. I said thank you so much sir. It's an honor to be working with you. He told them to sign me up. Everybody said no one addresses Mr. Arcan like that. I said look, he and I went to high school together. I said we are close friends.

Chapter 7

NASA

I began working with NASA at the Jet Propulsion Laboratory. One day we got the news that some special people called Spooks were coming to our laboratory and among them were members of the CIA such as Bill Corby, and The Shah of Iran. My boss and other members of our lab were there. From what I understand The Shah of Iran was offering our nation something like fifty billion barrels of oil every year for the protection of his nation. He wanted the United States of America to protect them so other nations wouldn't come in and take it from them. All of these people came to the lab. I was responsible for the lab and had to set up all the programs. We wanted to show them what we could do with data coming back especially because of the war with Vietnam. I stood in the background watching and listening to them talking. We were getting ready to put on the demonstration and lo and behold The Shah turns around, looking around the room, and looking directly at me said I want him to put the demonstration on. I was shocked. At that time, all eyes were on me.

Our boss got up and I sat down and put on the demonstration. I showed them that nothing could be hidden from our knowledge and that we could see through mountains and under the ground by adjusting our tools. The Shah was amazed at the capabilities of our laboratory. He was delighted. He thanked me and I thanked him. I told him it was a great honor to put the demonstration on for them. After they left our laboratory they went through the building to see what others were doing. My boss, Ron Workman, came up to me and said I was supposed to put on that demonstration because I am in charge. He was really ticked and walked out. The next day, he came back and said Pete I'm sorry, I was just a little upset. I said look Ron it doesn't matter who does the work in here, its team work. We need one another. Teamwork enables us to get images processed from the many satellite flights that we have to deal with here.

So many times people would have problems in the lab and I would work extra hours. I didn't ask them to pay me anything. I was getting paid with knowledge. If I didn't have to go to class or something like that I would go to work in the laboratory. I wanted to learn what they were doing. As I said knowledge is power. I think this is what really interfered with my married life to Gloria.

Gloria didn't like the idea that I worked so many late hours. She told me that if I didn't resign from NASA we would have to part. I had gone back and gotten the kids, and bought a house. I bought her a nice Ford with overdrive.

She had everything, including credit cards, and none of it made her happy. She wanted me home more often. I just couldn't leave NASA and the team. They were kind to me and I certainly reciprocated by being just as kind to them. Dr. Robert Nathan the chief scientist and Robert Seltzer were in charge of the laboratory. They said the images that we gathered (which were classified) using bit slicing technology for visual information, could be used for military purposes. We used to say there was no hiding place not even behind a mountain. We could take dark areas and remove them by using special techniques in our computer to see what was behind the mountain or under it. I remember when we had our flight to Mars and landed there. We had twelve VIP's in the lab looking at this spacecraft coming in. We used one microns transponder. We were always updating because when working with the government if we needed something there was no problem in getting it as far as money was concerned. It was just getting it there when we wanted it, and it had to be right.

Kinggo Kowano a Japanese engineer, was a great guy and I thought very highly of him. All the fellows there were great. We were supposed to update our system before this main flight to Mars and then sign off. It was something like $50 million dollars would be transferred from us to a company up in Silicon Valley that was doing the work for us. I looked over the circuit. In the horizontal deflection circuit they didn't have a protection where it would actually change the focus on the beam.

We had a real sharp one micron spark. If that sweeps collapsed, it would burn a hole right through a hundred million dollar tube that we were using to get sharp images. This tube gave us the ability to read license plates from that distance. That's how sharp it was. I said where's the deflection circuit? Where it is it? I kept saying this will never fly. My boss said what Pete? I said this will never fly. I won't sign off for this. Everyone was looking at me. My boss said Kinggo, is Peterson right about what he is saying or what? All the people that were there from General Precession and other big companies wanted to get their money on this unit they were selling to our lab. Kinggo looked over his glasses and said he's right, never will it fly, it would burn a whole right through. Sure enough they did a test flight and it did happen. It burned a hole. They had to fly a CR tube, the main tube, down because I had to put it back into our equipment. As large as our laboratory is the whole unit was something like eight feet tall and maybe fifteen or twenty feet long and I had to take all this apart to put the tube in it and line it back up which I did. I think it was just about an hour before ground zero. I worked twenty three hours straight to do it. It all lined up. When that spacecraft was right close to the ground of Mars, I took pictures of it showing us the foot paths landing on Mars (and the moon too).

I had the great honor of processing the Ranger, the Mariner, the Surveyor and the 109 day flight to Venus. According to what NASA and the people at JPL said it was only twelve of us who saw the landing on the moon.

My dear friends Dr. Robert Nathan and Robert Seltzer were in charge. I was there with them when the Ranger, our first spacecraft, landed on the moon and Armstrong our astronaut walked on the moon. They said to me, Peterson did you realize a great event happened here. I said yes and I'm so deeply honored to know that I could help you gentlemen in any way possible. They said no we know that; but do you realize what this means?

I said yes we landed the spacecraft on the moon and took images for processing. (Walter Cronkite, Dr. Picklin and all the VIP's from the lab were there to see the landing on the moon) And they said look Peterson, dog gone it, you're the first colored man in the world to see the moon's surface from less than a half a mile. They said that is really an honor. I said oh, yes that's right and I'm so thankful that we were successful. I was really happy but was very tired. I almost wanted to fall out on the floor and go to sleep. I was worn out after having worked twenty-three hours straight. I had to take a half a day off. I came in at noon because I was so tired I slept late. I will never forget all the wonderful flights we took and the wonderful people that I met while I was there. I saluted all of the men and women who were there. They were tops in my book.

It was really a wonderful experience working for NASA. They allowed me to go to college at night taking courses at UCLA. I would come back to the JPL at 6 a.m. in the morning and take courses on computers and other things NASA was coming forth with concerning new processing techniques.

I enjoyed working with the many fine men and women there to get our projects off the ground. We had a team that just couldn't lose. I spent many hours and much overtime to help the team reach far distance planets and see what was on them. It was truly a deep honor. My marriage suffered as a result of my working so hard and long at the lab. My first wife, Gloria Johns Peterson had a job at Huntington hospital. She was getting uptight that I wasn't home enough. The only thing I could tell her was just hold out for me, it won't be long before these experiments are over and I'll spend as much time as possible with you. She told me that she was going to have to introduce me to Zorro. I said what do you mean Zorro; the only one I know is a Mexican gentleman who rode a black and white pinto horse. She said you'll find out if you don't resign very shortly. I'll be forced to introduce you to the Zorro I'm telling you about.

Then one day I got a knock on the door and the man said are you George V. Peterson and I said yes that's correct. He said this is yours. He started walking away and our little black and white terrier started barking at him. I looked in the letter and I was subpoenaed to go to court for divorce proceedings. It really broke my heart to know that I would have to go through that. I just couldn't leave the job that I was doing, consequently we came down to the finally stages of the divorce. I found out who Zorro was. He was a judge down in Los Angeles and he was a terror from what I understood. He really downed men left and right and saw to it that they paid child support for their kids and alimony to their wife.

He would strip them down to bare bones almost. During the first meeting where they try to bring families back together again at all cost, Gloria said this just wouldn't work for us. She wanted to push the issue that I pay her alimony and the house note. I was giving up the house and everything that was in the house at that time. It was quite an ordeal. I knew that I wouldn't have my children anymore. I still worked at the lab and was still going to school taking courses. I didn't know until I was told later on that they were somewhat skeptical about how my mind was. They knew I loved my kids. I found out that Gloria had been interested in some fellow who owned a restaurant in Albuquerque, New Mexico. I met with her one time after we were just about through speaking to each other. She wanted to come back after two or three months and throw the divorce out. I said look you got what you wanted and you lost what you had. I said I gave you all the chances and I can't change now. I told her that she would survive and maybe do better than she ever could with me. I told her that I was probably a misfit for her. I reaffirmed to her that I would take care of all my responsibilities as I had always done. I told her to just take care of the children and that was it. We had to go through a final hearing. Gloria told my attorney the way she wanted things to go and was talking to the Judge as if she were in charge.

The Judge said I've got too many cases and I'm not going to argue with you all day. She was so hard on the judge that he shoved us down to District Seven for our case to be settled.

My lawyer, Mr. Charles Scarlet told me I was blessed. He told me whatever the judge says to you, you just say yes sir your honor. I don't care what it is you say that. He said we have been pushed down to Judge Broddy's courtroom. He said you remember when I took you over to Judge Broddy's ranch out in Lancaster with your children and they rode horses. I said yes I remember. He said well that's the one you're going to be talking to. I already talked to him in the back room. Whatever he says, you just say yes sir your honor. That's all I want you to say. Judge Broddy said you will pay child support. I said yes sir your honor. He said you will pay alimony to your ex-wife. I said yes sir your honor. He said you will have to pay one dollar to her every month and I said yes sir your honor. So every month I would send one dollar to her. It was really a blessing because got through it with only a few scratches. That was the end of my first marriage. I took on all responsibilities for my children and made sure they were taken care of. She went off and got married to the fellow from Albuquerque, New Mexico. They went to Hawaii and everywhere. They took off with my children. I didn't see my children for almost five years. When Gloria and I separated during my working at the Jet Propulsion Laboratory, I rented a room from Aunt Virginia. She took to me and I took to her. She traveled a lot going to see her folks in Pittsburgh, Pennsylvania. She also went to other places like Mexico and Europe. I would be there and watch the house for her. She was only about four miles from the Jet Propulsion Lab.

While working at JPL I had the sad experience of Aunt Virginia passing away. I had to look for another place to live. Everything I had I could pack into my station wagon and move. I was traveling very light. One of my friends Herb Wilson lived not more than two miles from the lab, over Double Gates Canyon. You could see the laboratory from the back of his house.

He told me to come on over. He said he owned another house and the people had moved out. He told me he had a couple of horses over there and it would help if I kept an eye on them for him. The house was right across the street from his house. Herb said we could do some good hunting. I said that sounds good. I was sleeping in this three bedroom house on a military camp cot. I could hear the mice running under my cot at night and the horses making noises. Most of his horses were raw Broncos. I believe he brought them from Utah and was breaking them. He was with the Black Calvary down in Ft. Watauga, Oklahoma. He knew horses very well. I was learning all I could about them through him. When we would go deer hunting in Long Pine, we traveled straight up Route *395.* It's funny because all the western movies were being done there and I was going up there deer hunting over the same trails. I had some experiences while deer hunting. I crossed the Sierra Nevada Mountains on horseback with Herb. It was really hard on the horses. I did not like hunting in warm weather. I was used to snow being raised in New York. The horse I was riding was named She Biscuit. She was a good Mare. She had been a trotter so she had some gait on her.

She could keep that gait up for hours and we covered a lot of ground. Herb had a horse with a blaze going down his face. He could handle him but I couldn't. He topped that mountain looking around to make sure that there were no rattle snakes or anything on the trail. When we hit the top of Sierra Valley Mountain the sign read 9700 feet. I said my Lord where are we going. It was about thirty-five miles riding one-way over the top of the mountain down to the Kern River. When you are there, you are deep in the wilderness. I remember Herb telling me this is one thing you've got to learn Pete, if you don't take care of her she won't take care of you. He told me how to take care of her. He said I had to take the bridle off her, the saddle off, rub her down, and feed her. He had dry food that we would use to feed the horses. It was packed and put in the saddle bags. They would also eat down by the Kern River because there was a lot of grass down there. I still didn't feel comfortable crossing the river on horseback.

I felt this was going to be some trip which it was. I told Herb that I would sit and watch the horses to make sure they wouldn't run off although they were tethered. You never know when a bear or mountain lion might come out and the horses run off and leave you. So, I kept my eye on them. One day we were fishing in the Kern River and my horse started acting up in the middle of the river. The water was up to her shoulders. I took my hat off and hit her on the side of her head. I said get up there if you drown we both are going to drown. She took off and right out that River she came.

I rubbed her down, fed her and she was happy. Herb said let's see if we can get a mule deer, so we split up. I went one way and he went the other. The terrain I took was rocky. As I went up the rocks I was looking very carefully where I put my feet and my hands because that was diamond back country and I was fully aware of that. I went up this big rock. I didn't have cowboy boots on. I had on military type boots. I jumped down from the rock and was looking out in front of me about ten feet or more to be sure when I jumped down I wouldn't jump on a diamondback. Lo and behold I heard a rattle. It sounded like an amplifier that had a hundred watts. I must have jumped ten feet in the air and boy thank

God I did. When I landed down in the flat spot, I took my rifle off my shoulder. I looked around and saw the biggest diamond back ever. I had not seen anything like it in a zoo. It was just him and me out there. There was nothing but pure air between us. He had a head that looked like a giant softball. He was down in his s-curve. I said I'm going to give him a lead hammer right now. Then I remembered I read about a guy that shot at a diamondback and his bullet ricocheted off a rock. The diamondback was locked on me. I thought to myself if I get bitten by that diamondback I will never get to the truck; maybe I'd be dead before I got back to camp. Anyway, I watched him as he crawled away. He looked like a long train going back in some rocks. When I got to the top of the hill I saw two big mule deer. It was a great experience crossing the Kern River and seeing that big diamondback. We didn't have any luck on that trip so we went home.

  I told Herb my saddle seemed like it was slipping all the time. He said no you're not leaning forward enough. He got off his horse and said I'm going to tie a knot and split reins them. You hang on to this; don't let go because if you do that horse might drag you all over these rocks. Some of those rocks on the trail we came down looked like they were an hundred pounds or more. We had to go back up that trail to get to the truck. We came up behind old Bob Lewis's pack station. We started heading back to the truck and I felt like I was slipping. I was going back, and back and I said Herb the saddle is slipping. I don't know what's wrong with it, it's not tight. That's when the whole thing happened. I fell backwards off that Mare. My foot was caught in the stirrup by those military boots which I will never wear again. There I was with her head bent back looking at me. She was waiting for me to make a move. She was going to kick the day lights out of whatever was in her way and boy I could tell that. My legs were in between hers and she was shivering. Herb said get the heck out of there George, she's gonna go crazy on you. He turned around and came back cautiously so as not to scare her, but that Mare took off. I lifted up and took the hit on the ground; fortunately it didn't break my back. I said I've got to get out of here. When I went to move I found my left leg was jammed in the stirrup. I was kicking trying to get my boot loose. I said a prayer and my dear Lord answered me.

  The stirrup popped off. When it popped off, I turned loose those reins and that Mare stood up on her hind legs. She tried to take off and Herb blocked her. I had a hoof come within two to three inches of my head. It went right through saddle bags that were tied to my saddle. Lord knows she just missed my head. I rolled out just in time because if she had stepped on my head with her weight I would have had it. I was really shook up. Herb brought her back and talked to her a little bit. I finally got to my feet and moved around. I was a bit sore. Herb said George that's it. We are going to walk around a little while and let her get over the nervousness. We could see she was still a little jittery.

He said from here on we are going to walk because I'm not going to be carrying you across the saddle of that horse. I had hoped we would be able to carry a deer. We took our time and walked all the way up to the top of Sierra Nevada Mountain. We sat for a while talking and rubbing She Biscuit. I finally got back into the saddle and we rode down side the mountain to our truck. Boy what a great feeling it was to get in that truck. We packed the horses up in the truck and drove back home again. Three times I almost got killed on that hunting trip. I said to myself well that's about it for me I won't be going hunting for a while.

Chapter 8

Giving Back

After about six and a half years of working with NASA I began to do community outreach and public relations work for them. I went to the east side where most Mexicans lived and the west side where most of the colored people lived.

I lectured children in high schools and the YMCA. NASA was kind to let me. They let me use the movies of what we were doing to show the children. I began to feel that I needed to leave Pasadena, California. I could not stop thinking about how good it was with the children and the wife when we were on good terms. I was still going to school at night. I thought it was time to move on to the Oakland area and I did. One day I received a letter from Mrs. Mae (Nana Beal) and Artie Beal. Nana Beal used to look after Georgette and Bobby for Gloria and I while we worked. After the divorce I was reluctant to go around them because it would bring back memories of my children, and me picking them up there. Artie was a real great guy. He reminded me of my dad. He was husky and short in stature. He had a machine shop. I loved to go there and was always trying to learn something from him. In this letter she wanted to know if I was angry at them because I never came by to see them.

I used to wash my clothes at a laundry mat just below their house so I decided to go and pay them a visit. When I got to their home, I knocked on the door and heard Nana Beal say, "Here comes my son."

When I walked in the house Mildred (who was to become my second wife) was washing windows. Nana Beal was her ex-mother-in-law and she loved to play bridge. She would have bridge parties and Mildred would do the cooking and everything for her. Although Mildred had divorced her son, they were still friendly and on good terms.

We were all like a big family. We got along very well. Later on, Mildred told me that she didn't know who Nana Beal was talking about when she said "here comes my son". Mildred said she thought it was her ex-husband and there I walked in. I never directly met Mildred that day. We were always missing each other like two ships at sea, close to each other but never meeting. When I did meet her I asked her where she was from and she said I'm from Washington, the State of Washington. She asked me where I came from. I told her I worked at the Jet Propulsion Lab processing data coming back from space craft. She had green eyes as green as a leaf on a plant, and they sparkled. She was reddish in color. I told her that it was really wonderful to meet her. Finally I told her that I had come by, the day that she was washing windows, to see Nana Veal and let her know that I was not angry with her. I was just hurt to know that my children were no longer being kept by her. I told Mildred that I loved the northwest terrain. It was entirely different from where I came from. There were mountains; and mountains grow on you. I said I'd like to see that her home town sometime. Well it seemed like I was attracted to her and she was attracted to me. After a while, Mildred Glass and I got married. We moved to Tacoma, Washington. Mildred's sister Lena and her husband Thad lived there. They owned a house up there and asked us to come and live with them. I felt sure I could find a job easily because of my background in computers, electronics and video. I did secure a job at the Pacific National Bank of Washington and worked there three years.

  The gentleman in charge was Dick Cline, a real great guy. He was from Madera, California. He thought highly of me and I thought highly of him. I worked and did everything I could do; staging all the programs that the bank had to run, and putting in IBM 360 and IBM 370 computers. I put in all their video recorders, air conditioners and other things. The job could not have been over a mile from the house. I would go up the hill to Center Street and I was at the bank. Mildred and I finally got a little place right down the street from Lena and Thad. It was very comfortable and we enjoyed living in the State of Washington. Mildred's brother owned a gravel pit down by the Wynoochee River. I used to going fishing and hunting. I would catch salmon, steel heads and other fish all the time. You could catch 20 or 30 pound salmon. You had to use the eight ounces of lead on the line to hold your bait down because the current was so swift. The Salmon were so strong they would swim up that thing anyway. When they were hooked, those eight ounces came up like a cork. They hardly knew it was on there. If you didn't have a heavy enough line they would be gone with all your rigging. I always rigged up properly. Mildred and I really enjoyed ourselves. One day at the bank as I was changing the computers around I was talking to my buddy Dick. I asked him how things were going; were the VIPs upstairs happy. He said they wanted him to draw a floor plan for the bank and show how the computers were going to be placed. He said he didn't know when he would get through; it was really going to tie him up.

I said that's quite a task. I didn't tell him but one time I studied to be an architect. I had a feeling that it would be helpful for me to learn. So, I took it upon myself to draw the floor plans and he didn't know it. I handed it to him; I had left a space down below for him to sign it. He said I just can't do that Pete; you drew these things. I said no this is a gift from me to you. This is to show my gratitude for your helping me to secure this job. I told him I wanted him to accept it and to write his name down. I said that as far as I knew he did it.

He said Pete why didn't you become an architect you did a beautiful job on this? He just couldn't get over the fact that I had done that for him. He was tops in my book. Dick Cline was always in my corner. I could ask him any kind of question and he would give me a direct, truthful answer. I had so many wonderful friends that I met in the northwest. I knew that sooner or later I might get a call from Uncle Sam and I would have to give Dick two weeks to get someone to replace me. I told him that I wouldn't leave him hanging. He said he understood and I really appreciated that. After working there for some time, the bank was shifting and they moved up to Seattle. They had a bus that carried some of the people from our bank up there. We would work from 2 o'clock p.m. until about 11 o'clock at night five days a week. It was during that time that I decided to go to trade school to study for my FCC license. I knew that would be valuable to me, which it was. I attended Tacoma Technical School to get my second class license. In four weeks I went up to Seattle and took the FCC exam.

You had to take the first, second, and third. You had to take a step at a time and come back to take the others. I took all three at one time. They told me no one does that. Eight hours later I staggered to my feet and I was finished. I went home. About one week later I came home from the bank and Mildred had my first class FCC license in the window of our home that we were in the process of buying. What a thrill that was. I was so happy and Mildred was too. I had secured an FCC license in one shot. I knew once I secured that license I could dictate and control my own destiny in life. I knew I was going to take the ship radar endorsement, which I did nine months later. This meant that I could work on any airline, in any airport, and on any ship of America or any allied ship, to help guide them with the radar systems. This was a licensing with a lot of power. There were engineers I knew who had taken the exam and did not pass it. Fortunately I was blessed by our Lord to be able to pass it. It took me to a lot of places I could not have gone. I had a license that very few people possessed.

I got a call from Ron Workman, my old boss at the Jet Propulsion Laboratory. He was now working for Ford WDL (Western Development Labs). He wanted me to come back there and work with him. He said look Pete you tell them you'll give them two weeks, and you're coming down here. We need you badly. I've already told the image processing lab staff that you could set everything up and get things rolling down here.

The Vietnam War was starting and some important work for our government was needed. So I said okay, Uncle Sam has called; I guess I'll be scooting on down there. I told Dick Cline at the bank about the telephone call and worked the two weeks and was gone. Mildred and I left Tacoma, Washington, and went to Santa Clara, California. We rented a house there and I started work at Ford WDL. My main job for Ford WDL was processing data that came from carriers in Vietnam and sending data back through satellites. It was very interesting and I had a lot of responsibilities getting the laboratory together. A lot of my old friends were there from the Jet Propulsion Laboratory. In 1975 the Vietnam War was coming to a close and that meant it was time for me to move on to better things. In fact, I was no longer employed at Ford WDL processing data. Fortunately there was an opening for an Electronic Instructor teaching computers at Alum Rock Technical School in San Jose, California. I applied for the position and was hired. Mrs. Halveto Lopez was the Director of the school. The school was in a storefront and was about ninety-eight percent Mexican boys and girls. Most of them were harvesting peaches south of us in the fields. They were good students however, most of them were illegal. The Instructor, Bob Rojas was getting paid very well. I worked under Bob who was a great electrical engineer. He started out in the Navy teaching Navy students the basics of electronics.

 We had Sylvia Carp who was from Brooklyn, New York, teaching Mathematics. I was teaching the Fundamentals of DC, AC, Complex AC problems, phrase relation in an AC environment, and AC in computers.

We developed quite a team at the school. We helped these children not only by teaching them. We also taught them how to handle themselves, and to be neatly dressed when they went on a job interview. We certainly did a beautiful job with them because some of the boys and girls went quite far career wise after graduating from Alum Rock Technical School.

I heard that one of our students, a Mexican boy, had started stealing hub caps and smoking (KJ's) little marijuana cigarettes. When I saw him, I got a hold of him and tried to straight him up. I said look son, you've got a good head on your shoulders and I'll do all I can to help you; I want you to start doing what's right. I told him that since he had almost completed the course I wanted him to go and take the exam at Lockheed Martin and see what he could do. He aced that test. It turned out that they offered him a job making $12.75 an hour. This was the most money he had ever made on any job. He turned that job down to go to work for Hewlett Packard who was paying $9.75 an hour. It must have been about two or three days later that two of the executives that hire super technicians for Lockheed Martin came down to Alum Center. These executives heard that our student turned down a job with them making $12.75

and took a job with Hewlett Packard for $9.75. I told them that it wasn't just a job; Hewlett was giving him four years of college free. I asked them what were they giving him, only $12.75 an hour and maybe in a year he gets laid off. I have always taught that money isn't everything, and with knowledge you can dictate and control your own destiny in life.

I maintained that teaching all my life to all the students I taught. The executives from Lockheed said we went all the way down to Devry Technical School to bring our student back to work with them.

I said, "Gee, you go out 1500 miles rather than to look here in San Jose." I said, " I pray you will pick some boys and girls from our school." I told them they have great students right here in their backyard. I said that our students had the mind and skills to become invaluable to any company they go to work for. I told them that I also encouraged our students to go to college at night for telecommunication and computers. We put our students on the road to success in life. Sometimes I had to crack the whip to get them squared away. I did not allow playing around in my classes. My students knew when they stepped into the arena they had to be ready or they'd get knocked out and I would have someone else to fill their chair. I didn't have time for people that were going to fool around and interrupt my class schedule. Alum Rock School had some good boys and girls. They just needed someone to stand in their corner, reprimand them when needed, and run a tight ship as I call it. All the boys and girls thought very highly of me at the Alum Rock School. We had these cards that we had to fill out to show the attendance records. I said look I'm getting sick and tired of you coming here with these soiled cards from here on out I want your cards clean. I noticed that after an hour or more all the children seemingly had to go to the restroom, boys and girls. Bob Rojas came in my classroom and said George what happened.

I said, "I don't know I guess they all got sick or something. I don't know what's going on maybe you can find out. " He talked to a couple of them that were walking out and they said no we can't stay any longer Mr. Peterson said he wants our green cards and a lot of us don't have green cards.

He said they thought you were requesting their green cards when you said you want their clean cards. He had to explain to them what I meant. I really thought the world of those boys and girls. At that time I smoked a pipe, which I picked up from my grandfather. The students would come outside and ask me; how come you come out here and we see you smoke a pipe and it looks like your mind is so far away. I would say well it is sometimes. They asked why do you smoke it.

I told them I smoked a pipe because a pipe draws wisdom from the lips of a philosopher and shuts the mouth of a fool. They said oh you're a professor. I said no I just like speakers of the truth no matter who it hurts. The greatest speaker of the truth in the world is our Lord Jesus Christ who we all love. I pray even in school that you will learn to know and love Him if you haven't as yet. They said I just can't believe you're a professor you never said anything like that. They would say pro-fes-sor. I would say no. They would say oh yes you are. Those children would not stop calling me professor. I said okay whatever you say. They would ask me questions when I would be outside on break smoking my pipe. Their questions would be about philosophy and other things; like why you do this, why you do that, what do you say about this or that.

I would ask them the same questions back again to see how they thought and what level they were on. I really loved all the students. It made me happy to see how far they had come from where they started. The word spread like wildfire. Alum Rock School students were acing all their tests and were being offered jobs paying more than they had made in their lives. I taught them that if they had knowledge they had power and you could dictate and control your own destiny in life. It was in the beginning of January and it was getting close to honoring our Rev. Dr. Martin Luther King Jr. The students asked who he was. I said he's the man. Dr. Martin Luther King Jr. is very similar in comparison to Poncho Villa. He was struggling for his nation like we are here. Black Americans have been struggling to have full class citizenship, this is our country too. We fought for this nation and we have received nothing so far. I said I pray that one day a Black man will become the president. They said maybe you can take time out and explain who Poncho Villa was and how similar his background was to Dr. Martin Luther King's. I was told by Mrs. Lopez that I could not stop teaching class curriculum to teach on Dr. King and Poncho Villa. She said that could not happen and I got the shock of my life. Those children went to the office and said if you don't allow the professor to tell us about Poncho Villa and Dr. Martin Luther King we're going to walk out this school right now.

All of them were standing there with their hats and lunch boxes in their hands ready to go out.

She came back begging me to talk to them. I said look, it'll take me only about a half an hour max and they'll make it up by doing real well in quizzes. I would be deeply honored to do this for them. So, on Martin Luther King's Day I wrote this poem:

POEM TO ALUM ROCK SCHOOL STUDENTS RE: MLK JR.

Today we all honor the death of a great citizen of our country, Rev. Dr. Martin Luther King Jr.; yet I feel that he is not dead but in a deep sleep; for his deeds and wonderful thoughts will always live on in the hearts and minds of all men and women of color who are striving for the equal rights that our constitution has granted to all its citizens.

If one pauses a moment they can visualize a similarity to the struggles of a past great man south of our borders in Mexico during the early 1900's who like Rev. King, <u>HAD A DREAM</u> that the poor in his country would receive their equal rights too.

This great proud man, Poncho Villa, like Rev. Dr. Martin Luther King, Jr. will never be forgotten, but should be instilled deep not only in our minds and heart but in those of our children and young people who must always carry this burning torch in their minds and hearts.

Rev. King's death has given us all, who are living today a new birth with not only the idea's and philosophies at his death, but new ones to help the poor and the uneducated people of this great and wonderful country to gain their equal rights. We all must understand that our new birth is but a sleep and a forgetting. The soul that rises with us - our life star- hath had elsewhere its setting and cometh from a far.

For not our brother Rev. Dr. Martin Luther King Jr. who is now our life star.

Tell me and I forget.

Teach me and I remember.

Involve me and I learn.

After my speech, the students just clapped and clapped and clapped. You could hear them out in the streets. They were loud and excited about the poem and me. We put a lot of wind in those children's sails; how I thought so well of them. I still think of them. I will never forget them. They were wonderful. These are the words inscribed on the beautiful plaque they gave me below.

Thank You George V. Peterson In appreciation for putting our Butterflies in <u>Formation</u> The Tech classes and Staff for Center Employment Training

THE END

CPSIA information can be obtained
at www.ICGtesting.com
Printed in the USA
BVHW041815020120
568398BV00012B/395/P

9 781494 447434